SONGS
OF THE
ROOD

VOLUME I

Centenary Chronicles of the
Sisters of the Holy Cross

SONGS
OF THE
ROOD

A CENTURY OF VERSE BY
SISTERS OF THE HOLY CROSS

Saint Mary's of the Immaculate Conception
Notre Dame, Holy Cross, Indiana

Volume I

PS
591
.C3
S48

SAINT ANTHONY GUILD PRESS
PATERSON, NEW JERSEY

FOREWORD

THE precedent for verse in religious life is continuous. It includes the greatest poetry in the world. It includes much that is not great, much that is scarcely more than devotional verse. But the tradition is wholly glorious and apocalyptic. Coventry Patmore has said: "The poet always treats spiritual realities as the concrete and very credible things they truly are. . . . All realities will sing, but nothing else will." This perception of spiritual realities in things of sense is the essence both of poetry and of the life of the mind and the soul.

The sustained practice of verse writing in the Community of the Holy Cross is a commentary on the reality of its spiritual life. It is a revelation of its capacities for contemplation, for poetry is the heaven of contemplative thought. The quality of much of this verse is a matter of genuine and varied poetic gifts. This fact also is significant, a delicate mark of God's favor and trust.

Whatever their mere artistic value, these hundred songs gathered across a century reveal in one way the sight and insight, the singing strength of the Sisters of the Holy Cross. Simply, unequivocally, they speak the love and dedication of an entire community, a corporate love and dedication in which the identity of the individual singers is gladly lost.

An anthology is literally a collection of flowers. Like flowers, these verses have been gathered from a score of blossoming garden plots. Like flowers, they are for remembrance. A hundred years from now they may still be quaintly, subtly sweet with a perennial fragrance of God.

SISTER M. MADELEVA

ACKNOWLEDGMENTS

Grateful acknowledgment for permission to reprint some of these poems is made to the editors of *America, Annals of Our Lady of Lourdes, The Bengalese, The Catholic Apostolate, The Catholic World, Columbia, Commonweal, Extension Magazine, The Franciscan,* the *New York Sun, Saint Anthony's Messenger* and *Spirit.*

CONTENTS

CONTENTS

X

CONTENTS

CONTENTS

CONTENTS

SONGS
OF THE
ROOD

RECOMPENSE

I BAKE white sheets of wheaten bread
  And sunder them apart;
Each wafer holds my finger prints
  Where soon will beat His heart.

I count the hosts by thousands;
  In each I shrine my plea,
And now my cares are sacred trusts
  For all eternity.

SISTER M. ANSELMA

IN BEAUTY HE IS CLOTHED

IN BEAUTY He is clothed today,
The beauty of our mortal clay;
The Lord is clothed in strength, for He
Put on our frail humanity,
When in His mother's womb He lay.

The cold, the pain, the shadows gray
Of loneliness that mark life's way
Brought even love to misery
   In Bethlehem.

But now around His bed of hay,
Where mother-maid and Joseph pray,
Adoring angels bend their knee,
And shepherds worship when they see
The Babe, a God from heaven, astray
   In Bethlehem.

SISTER M. ANTONINE

ALONE WITH GOD

Alone with God! through all my days
To see the beauty of His ways:
To know Him in the dawn's faint light,
To feel His touch in sunbeams bright
That lift the distant mountain haze.

On every fragrant breeze that sways
The roses into songs of praise
My soul is lifted to love's height
    Alone with God!

In after years when strength decays,
When faith grows dim, and hope betrays,
Should sorrow veil Him from my sight,
I'll seek Him through the starless night,
And on the tabernacle gaze
    Alone with God!

SISTER M. ANTONINE

THE QUEST

WHERE lies the road to Bethlehem,
  The royal House of Bread?
A narrow road, a rugged road,
  Leads to a cattle shed.

Where watch the shepherds through the night,
  Their lonely vigil keep?
The starlit plains beyond the town
  Are white with sleeping sheep.

Where speed the angels in their flight
  On wings of love aflame?
The hills have caught their song of peace
  And echo back His name!

Where lies the Son of God in state?
  His mother's veil withdraw.
Behold! His throne, a manger bare,
  His crown, a wisp of straw.

I found the road to Bethlehem,
  The shepherds poor, the shed,
Adoring angels, peace and God
  Within His House of Bread!

SISTER M. ANTONINE

IN ADVENT

She comes, and lo! it is the dawn!
 Behold the day arise!
The shadows of the night are gone;
 I see sweet Mary's eyes.

MOTHER M. BARBARA

HYMN OF PRAISE

ALL days are God's, and each successive dawn
Is but a note that swells the hymn of praise
Which incense-like from earth to heaven ascends,
And thither bears the soul's deep gratitude
To God, the Source whence every blessing flows.

SISTER M. BERTILDE

IMAGES

I STOOD upon a singing streamlet's marge
Unkissed of skiff or barge,
And saw an ashen boulder palely gleam
Within the glassy stream,
Cleaving the murmuring brooklet's silken flow
To myriad lights below,
Until from out the boulder's stony heart
The waters seemed to start.
Then swift arose before my musing ken,
In desert wastes untrod,
The streams that burst at Moses' smiting rod.
Then, as I gazed, the sun its beams divine
Poured down like golden wine,
And broken ripples, catching amber gleams,
Seemed liquid light of dreams,
Or from the darkling rock took happy flight,
Gay butterflies of light!

SISTER M. BLANCHE

TO KEATS

Snatched in life's flower away
Ere broke thy laureled day,
Ere from thy spirit strong
Burst half its prisoned song,

Thou didst the great world-heart
Win by thy matchless art;
What though thy days were brief,
What though surcharged with grief?

Now o'er thine alien grave,
Hard by the Tiber's wave,
Oft to the Roman sky
Riseth the pilgrim sigh.

Honor and deathless fame
Halo thy magic name;
Ah! not "in water writ" —
Graved on our hearts is it!

Builder of lofty rhyme,
Mage of the art sublime,
Marble to dust may fly;
Thy verse can never die.

SISTER M. BLANCHE

8

FROM BONDAGE FREE

Firmly around the mountain's lonely crest
   The glittering glacier's icy arms were flung;
It drank the starbeams; o'er its frozen breast
   A silver splendor hung.

And far above, the sky's deep bell of blue,
   Sprinkled with glistening pollen-dust of stars,
Hung like a harebell graced with golden dew
   When morn her gate unbars.

Nor moon's soft argent floor, nor starry dart
   The glacier pierced, until the wooing sun
Upon it smiled, when lo! its death-cold heart
   By summer warmth was won.

Then down the mountain took their laughing way
   A thousand streamlets from ice-bondage free,
Singing and leaping in their liquid play
   Into the heaving sea.

As oft in anthem grand the singers hold
   A momentary discord — then along
The slope of silence run like molten gold
   Rare, rapturous rills of song.

SISTER M. BLANCHE

9

SURSUM CORDA

Sweet perfume from the lilies reaches me;
Their beauty telling of a holier land
Lifts up my thoughts, as waves to distant strand
Bear floating waifs from out a troubled sea.
Like silent angels in humility
Low bending, as if blessed by Jesus' hand,
They cluster round His shrine. Ah, happy band!
Unknown to toil, they yield Him homage free.

Thus with a master touch, the lilies fair
With beauty gently waken our deep souls,
Their message bringing; on the quiet air
Wave after wave of breathing sweetness rolls,
Clear voices calling us to God; while prayer
Guides us toward Him, safe through myriad shoals.

SISTER M. CHERUBIM

MORNING PRAYER AT OLD FAITHFUL

From out the heart of mother earth
   White prayers arise.
Like myriad censers, mute in praise,
   They reach the skies;
While lordly pines in reverence wait
   The morning sacrifice.

Accept, dear Lord, this gracious morn
   Our word of love,
Which blends with nature's orison
   To Thee above.

SISTER M. DOLOROSA

THE HEIGHTS

ONLY the highest mountain peaks
   Are lit by the early sun;
Down in the sleeping valley
   The day has not begun.

Only the waiting, eager heart
   Can recognize God's light;
Souls earthbound ever dormant lie
   In selfish shades of night.

SISTER M. DOLOROSA

NEARING HOME

THE evening clouds are drifting to the west;
    White sails float softly on a radiant sea;
So lulled to peace with thoughts of coming rest,
    Dear Lord, my soul is nearing home and Thee.

The night of life was long; the tempest wild
    Bore down in fury on my fragile bark;
My faint heart grieved, O Saviour, meek and mild,
    I feared that I had lost Thee in the dark.

But Thou wast nearer, nearer than I thought;
    The dark waves brightened like a sudden flame;
And in Thy arms I found the peace I sought
    As I in anguish called upon Thy name.

The storm is over and the night has gone;
    With childish trust I clasp Thy guiding hand
And turn my face toward the winds of dawn,
    Blown from the green shores of the fatherland.

SISTER M. DOLOROSA

EXCHANGE

I AM all Thine, Beloved, for
I come
Unbound and free;
Now I am stripped of everything
I love
To love but Thee;
Of everything, and yet, my Lord,
I have
Fair memory.

The wide world is my home; but once
I knew
A garden close,
And sheltering walls encircled by
The press
Of rambling rose.
In every soul that I may help
My heart
A new home knows.

And once when all my life was young
I dreamt
Of little feet,
And tiny hands and rosy mouth;
Ah! Lord,
Those dreams were sweet!

Today a thousand little hands
Await
My love to meet.

And in this dream of yesterday,
The whole
Wide world was mine.
I held it close against my heart;
But now
A love divine
Has given more than life can give,
Himself,
The Bread and Wine.

SISTER M. DOROTHY ANN

ARTISTRY

OF WHAT strange matter has God made the girl,
Elusive as the dews that shaggy hedges pearl
Before they melt within the kisses of the sun.
She is a golden dream but half begun,
A fairy leading through alluring ways,
With all the fragrant morning in her gaze.
She is the laughter of all noonday skies,
The sudden mist of tears in evening's faded eyes.
She is the sigh from passing sadness sprung,
A song of life with all its lines unsung.
She is the mother of a race to be,
The molder of a nation's destiny.
She is a white seed prisoned in a stirring clod,
Spirit and earth. What whimsy in the mind of God
To make the girl and let her young hands hold
All flowers of love and life as they unfold!

MOTHER M. ELEANORE

16

THE LESSON

I HAD not known what life might be,
Until death came to talk with me.

But now I know the reason why
The brave white stars are riding high.

I know why grass wants rain, and how
The eager twigs reach from the bough

To catch the sun; why April spills
Her bright young laughter down the hills.

My ears are tuned to the strong whir
Of a bird's wings. I feel the stir

Of restless seeds within the earth.
The crying of a child at birth

Smites me to ecstasy. I know
The throb of water's undertow.

I love my pulse beats and swift breath,
Since I have had my talk with death.

MOTHER M. ELEANORE

17

SON, BEHOLD THY MOTHER

As JESUS went about His quiet ways,
Those thirty years from helpless infancy
To man's estate, He fashioned secretly
A gift too beautiful to touch with praise.
He Who had but to speak to set ablaze
A million suns, for bread toiled patiently,
That He might as His chosen artistry
Devise and shape through loving nights and days.

But three years spent He saving all the world,
Building a Church too strong for hell to harm,
Forgiving, casting fires of faith that curled
Through pagan dark, compelling men by charm
To love. Yet thirty years He set apart
To form the beauty of one woman's heart.

MOTHER M. ELEANORE

18

PETER

Prince of Apostles

He whom Christ made the head
Of all His kingdom on the earth, one day
Bethought him of his home, his nets, his pay,
And to Christ said,
"We have left all for Thee."
Pleasant was news of promised hundredfold,
Of seat as judge; not yet could he be told
Of scourge and tree.

At the Fire

He whom Christ gave the fire
He cast upon the earth, to kindle and
To tend, came with the crowd one night to stand
Where those whose hire
Was merely money kept their fires aglow
To warm the outer court; and for warmth he
Stayed on, tempting so much his custody,
His fire died low.

WITH THE BELOVED

He whom Christ told to feed
His lambs and sheep, one night struck with his sword
A wolf that dared the sheepfold of the Lord —
The Lamb had need,
He thought, of him. Then came
The day when, humbled, he the Shepherd heard
Ask not for sword but for one tender word,
Three times, the same.

SEVENTY TIMES SEVEN

He whom Christ gave the keys
Of heaven, asked what measure should be used
For pardons given or for those refused:
Should mercy cease
At once, or count to seven?
And then he learned that men's poor little minds
Can never count the number and the kinds
Of keys to heaven.

In the Mamertine Prison

He whom Christ called a rock
Struck the rock floor and saw a stream arise,
Wherewith in dungeon dark he could baptize
His last, small flock.
And when a soldier's hand
Struck that old head against the thick stone wall,
It graved a likeness that still says to all,
"The rock will stand."

On the Cross

He whom Christ set above
All men, with height could not be satisfied,
So lowly was he since he had denied
His own dear Love;
Hence, he was raised so high
Above the world upon two beams of wood,
That, looking down, he visioned that he stood
Upon the sky.

THE FISHERMAN OF SOULS

He whom Christ gave the right
His fellow-men to bind or to set free,
Could not himself from chains of memory
Free day or night;
As by his fisher's hook
His victim was pulled in, so all his years
He was drawn up through endless floods of tears
By one brief look.

MOTHER M. ELEANORE

22

REMEMBRANCE

I FOUND the first spring violet today
And took it in my hand
To bring it home to you,
Smiling to think how you would say:
"You dainty elf from fairyland
In gown of blue,
Your breath brings all the woodland and the spring
Here to my room, and I forget how tired I am of pain!"
Eager, I hurried on my way — then suddenly
Against my heart I crushed the fragile thing.
How vain
Such haste! I could not see
The path I trod.
Yet, with the sweet insistence of its breath
The broken thing against my heart — blue,
Like the eyes of you —
Whispered that broken things are dear to God,
And told me that through joys you know since death
Its flower-soul would waft my love-thought, too.

MOTHER M. ELEANORE

CANDLES

Dᴇᴀʀ, I have lit a candle for your birthday,
Because a candle is so like to you.

There is no need of candles in the sunshine;
There is no need of love when life is gay.
But a small candle set within a window
When twilight brings its shadows cold and gray
Tells of a mother waiting with her dearness
To comfort hearts the day has touched with pain.
A little candle shining from a window
Sends hope serenely through the wind and rain.

Dear, I have lit a candle for your birthday;
Death cannot keep your love from shining through.

MOTHER M. ELEANORE

IRISH, PLEASE ANSWER

OH, WHERE were all the fairies I had longed to see today?
I sought them in the purple mists above the Dublin bay.
I watched for them in the young winds that jigged up
    from the south,
To make their tender mischief in the solemn trees of
    Howth.
I searched amid the heather starred with flecks of gorse's
    gold,
And scanned the backs of tethered goats with faces wise
    and old.
I brushed the hedge, but to alarm all sorts of flying things,
And looked in vain for them upon the sailboats' wide
    white wings.
I sought them on the waves that dance below fair Ire-
    land's Eye,
And listened for their laughter through the seagull's
    lonely cry —
Perhaps it was the boldness of the sun kept them away:
'Tis said they dance by moonlight and are seldom seen
    by day.
And yet somehow tonight, within my bedroom's narrow
    walls,
Where light is garish and where sound but rasping city
    calls,
I look at sprigs of heather and I chill with sudden fear
Lest from this stolen treasure a wild fairy face should
    peer.

MOTHER M. ELEANORE

ASSUMPTA EST MARIA

Angels clad thee in a vesture
Woven from thy virtue's gold,
When with crown of pearls the richest,
Set with gems of priceless worth,
They adorned thee, and all hailed thee
Queen of angels and of earth.

Queen of earth as well as heaven,
Look on me, thy sinful child,
On this day of thy Assumption,
Vestal of the undefiled.
Reign, O Queen, o'er all my actions;
Guard my heart and keep it pure;
Shelter me beneath thy mantle;
There I'll rest fore'er secure.

SISTER M. EVARISTA

26

THE STAR OF BETHLEHEM

Behold the kings, their toilsome journey o'er,
In rapture kneel before the Babe divine!
In Him they see the mystic radiance shine
That guided them afar from orient shore
Through desert's weary stretch, o'er fen and moor
And mountain height. He bears no royal sign,
This King of kings; but prostrate they incline
And at His little feet their treasures pour.

O faith's sweet light! unerring guiding star!
No gloom can e'er your radiance overwhelm.
Us too you lead from doubting darkness far
Unto the Eucharistic Bethlehem;
There you reveal to our adoring eyes
Our Lord concealed 'neath love's most lowly guise.

SISTER M. EVARISTA

CRYING HIS NAME

His voice I hear amid these kingly trees;
   His smile is in the sunlight on the sea.
Lo! everywhere each perfect flower and leaf
   Cries out His name and limitless love for me.
I see His beauty in the fair white sands
   Cast in divine profusion on the shore;
And when I walk in the deep forest glades
   I find His footprints on the shadowed floor.

SISTER M. FRANCESCA

COMPENSATION

Together now we cannot walk the ways
We grew to love. The stars will glow and die
Upon the southern skies, but you and I
Shall lonely vigil keep through all the days.
Bright fields of blue in spring we cannot share;
Gay morn and pensive evening we shall miss,
Sweet interchange of sorrow and of bliss,
And simple things our friendship rendered fair.

But we can walk together Calvary's height
And watch with Mary by the holy cross;
Deep peace will fill the emptiness of night
And Love Himself will compensate for loss,
When at the early dawn, though worlds apart,
We come to meet at worship in His heart.

SISTER M. FRANCESCA

SONG FOR A WAKEFUL NIGHT

I SHALL lie quiet here until the dawn
When I have tryst to keep with Christ my King.
O consecrate hour is this to dwell upon,
The miracle that wings of day will bring.
Beyond the dark, sound of His feet I hear,
And in me burns adoring faith whereof
Across the span of night my soul shall rear
A shining arch of triumph for my love.

I used to fear the watches of the night
And longed for sleep to heal the wounds of day,
But now the shadows hold a dear delight
And silence has deep mysteries to say.
All yearnings for my God upgathered are,
Desire illumes the darkness like a star.

SISTER M. FRANCESCA

MAGNIFICAT

Sing to our Lady, O sea,
A hymn of praise for me;
Lift your white waves to the sky,
Sign of her purity.
Sweep your blue waters far
Out of love for the Morning Star.
O sing to her without spot
One long Magnificat!

SISTER M. FRANCESCA

DIVINE IMPRESS

Desolate, blind with tears, you sought your way
Amid the rabble and the sudden dark
That told His dying, not the end of day.
I think in that black hour you did not mark
The priceless gift that in your hands you bore.
Only at last within your own firelight
You knelt in rapturous silence to adore
His image etched in blood on veil of white!

Veronica! so may it be with me.
Though on this paltry thing I weave of life,
Only a clash of colors I can see,
A faltering, ill-shaped pattern in the strife,
His love may leave, however dim, a trace,
A touch of beauty, impress of His face.

SISTER M. FRANCESCA

SUFFERING

Are your lips almost dumb?
He is pleading you come
And hear only His voice.
Are you weary of pain?
Ask to feel it again
For the love of your Lord.
Is your soul steeped in grief?
He once begged for relief
In a garden alone.
Voice a prayer in your heart
For your glorious part
Of a child at His feet.
Sing a song in your soul
For this mystical role
Of the suffering Christ.

SISTER M. FRANCES EUGENE

ANTICIPATION

IF I could look with clearest eye and see
The windings and the roughness of the road
That lie beyond; if I could feel the load
Of weariness that each new year will be
Upon me laying; could I but foresee
The daily words and acts unkindly stowed
And reap the harvest of the pain they sowed:
With such a vision, could life stay in me?

Dear God, I render fervent thanks to Thee
For mercy which has hidden from my eye
The future's daily cross and misery.
Thy Son knew all and suffered more thereby.
I ask Thee not to ope tomorrow's door
But grace to bear each cross and love Thee more.

SISTER M. FRANCES EUGENE

SONG

O GOLDEN linnet, with your tiny feet
Alight upon a thistle bloom, each note
On fragrant summer's scented breath afloat
Is mingled with it, crystal-clear and sweet
As dew on flowers. With you I dare compete,
O singer in the black and yellow coat,
Whose molten music from a golden throat
Pours out. My song with joy is more replete.

The ripple of the brook is in your song,
The silver splash of rain, a love-note low,
And yet it lacks a song's most precious thing,
A soul. O sing through all the summer long!
The greater gift is mine. You cannot know
Who hears your song, who taught you how to sing.

SISTER M. GENOVEVA

MASS

You ask: What is the Mass to me?
My hour to stand on Calvary.

And this is why I love it so:
It is my way to let Him know

Had I been there, then I had stood
That time beneath the shameful rood,

As now beneath the mystic tree
Where He renews the mystery.

And I am glad of this strange thing,
He finds my presence comforting.

SISTER M. GENOVEVA

ARCHERS OF THE KING

TIME was, no archer with impunity
Pierced my proud armor. Never arrow flew
But passed its mate midway. Whose livery
The bowman wore I took no heed, nor knew
What master artisan with faultless craft
Had forged the arrows, till one hour of stress
When stricken sore, I drew the splintered shaft
And found engraven on it, I. H. S.

O Arrow-Maker with the wounded hands,
My bitterness is shattered into tears,
And now at length my dull heart understands
The need of pain. I wait the coming years
With empty quiver and a slackened string,
Disarmed before the archers of the King.

SISTER M. GENOVEVA

RECOMPENSE

God saw me watching Him one winter night
When He was making silhouettes of trees
Against a crimson sky. For my delight
He paused to bid a light, soft-fingered breeze
Unveil the moon. God found me in the spring
Attending on His footsteps, standing by
Where violets grew, while for my marveling
He waked from sleep a gold-winged butterfly.

For that I loved His work, He came to give
His touch of beauty where my soul had been
Long since in need of it; so now I live
Content to see His quiet work within,
And sometimes when I watch Him wistfully,
He turns to ask some little help from me.

SISTER M. GENOVEVA

SPENDTHRIFT

A SPENDTHRIFT youth, Assisi's gayest lad
In joyous giving spent his father's gold,
The princely Francis in rich velvet clad,
A merchant's son with soul of kingly mould.
"A fool," said Bernardone. "He has no care
For gain, and even of his spirit's bliss
He could not keep the whole, but needs must share
And press it on a leper with a kiss."

His father's storehouse barred, he pilfered love,
And filled his heart from heaven's treasury.
Then since he heard no censure from above
He gave to all earth's children lavishly;
Nor thieves, nor woodland creatures thought too low,
He shared it with the wolf of Gubbio.

SISTER M. GENOVEVA

39

VISION

You scorn this brown cocoon! Oh, if you knew
The vision that it holds of moonlight things,
The drifting through soft air of pale green wings,
A connoisseur delighting all night through
To sip from fragrant flower-cups of dew
The honeyed wine! No treasure chest of kings
Holds half the joy this little brown case brings
To me. And in such wise God loves us, too.

Unlovely often to our half-blind eyes,
So seems our neighbor in his house of clay.
We see the crudeness, the unpleasant way,
Then hold him up for judgment, and despise
Where God Himself most loves, because He sees
Within his soul the hidden sanctities.

SISTER M. GENOVEVA

THE REASON

Saint joseph was a silent saint;
  He scarcely spoke a word.
And yet his heart was wondrous full
  Of secrets he had heard.

Saint Joseph was a gentle man,
  And near, should Mary call.
His listening soul was speechless
  With the wonder of it all.

SISTER MARY HELEN

41

THE SINGING MAIDEN

I WOULD not trade my little gift
   For wealth of any king;
When I am glad, when I am sad,
   My simple heart can sing.

Sometimes I sing of laughter;
   Sometimes I sing of tears;
And I shall keep on singing
   Through all the years.

When I come to heaven,
   If I must stand and wait,
I'll sing the gladdest song I know
   Outside the gate.

And kindly old Saint Peter
   The door will open wide
And ask, "Who is this happy soul
   I've kept outside?"

My song in great high heaven
   Scarce anyone will hear,
But my most gracious mother
   Will lend her ear.

And leading me before the throne,
"My Lord," the queen will say,
"Another singing maiden
Would honor Thee today."

SISTER MARY HELEN

IDENTITY

SHOULD you meet a little saint
　　Abroad in heaven town,
Shy and sweet and gentle,
　　In a modest gown;

Should you find her worrying
　　About such things
As broken harp cords
　　Or bruised wings;

Should you see her glancing
　　Down toward earth,
Then she is the mother
　　Who gave me birth.

Should she pluck for daisies
　　The loveliest stars,
And when Peter isn't looking
　　Let down the bars

So that all the sinners
　　May quietly slip in
That God may forgive them
　　And wash away their sin;

Should she seem uneasy
　　When Michael wields his sword,
Then she is my mother,
　　The handmaid of the Lord.

Should you see her watching
   With an anxious air
As every newcomer
   Mounts the golden stair,

Eager and expectant,
   She's hoping to see
A ragged little sinner
   Looking like me.

Should you see her wandering
   Far out of sight,
Pray do not blame her,
   Heaven is so bright,

And she, little gray bird,
   Seeks a quiet nest
Among the birds and flowers
   Where she may rest

Until all her children
   Are safely home at last,
And the days of waiting
   And sorrow are past.

Should you chance to meet her,
   Tell her, my friend,
That we love and need her
   World without end.

SISTER MARY HELEN

THE BURIAL

JOSEPH, keep your linen fine;
He has no need for cloth of thine.
He, the King's Son, has a shroud
Of color proud, like purple wine.

The seamless robe made by His mother
They took away. He wears another,
Fashioned softly on the loom
Of her womb to give Him cover.

His diadem, it is most rare:
Blood-red the rubies in His hair.
A filigree of crimson lace
Hides His face and hands so fair.

Women, it was kindly thought,
But needless are the spices brought.
Scent the fragrant roses sweet
In His feet so finely wrought.

With water would you wash Him clean?
On the height have you not seen
Him laved in water from His side
Open wide, where love has been?

I pray you, do not bury Him!
That were task for seraphim.
See how quietly He sleeps
While Mary weeps at sight of Him.

SISTER MARY HELEN

PETITION

ONCE on a journey,
Weary Your feet,
You met Your mother
On a crowded street.

With arms extended
She uttered a cry;
Long You gazed at her
Passing by.

When You meet my mother,
Will You comfort her?
She too has known sorrow
And the taste of myrrh.

She has stood on Calvary
Beneath a leaden sky;
Without a murmur
Watched her child die.

She is bound to duty
As to a cross;
Faces life bravely,
Counts gain a loss.

When You meet my mother,
Will You comfort her?
She too has known sorrow
And the taste of myrrh.

SISTER MARY HELEN

THE LISTENER

THERE is a little lady,
Not a word can she hear;
God closed the sound-box
  In her ear.

She is an artist
With colors and words;
They praise God gaily
  As singing birds.

Sometimes I envy
The things she hears,
While the world clamors
  At my ears.

Her eyes grow starry;
Her gentle lips smile;
She sits chatting
  With Jesus awhile.

This other Mary
Chose the better part;
She sits listening
  With her heart.

SISTER MARY HELEN

EPIPHANY

BEHOLD, I come!
Come like the Magi
From afar,
Led by the light
Of faith, a star,
To where a host
Of virgins are
About a King.
For gifts I bring:
My poverty,
Which gives to me
His wealth untold;
My chastity,
Which makes me free
His love to hold;
My liberty,
More dear to me
Than love or gold.

SISTER MARY HELEN

OUR LADY OF THE SACRED HEART

O HEART of Mary, crystal spring
Of purity and love divine,
My tired, erring heart I bring.
O wilt thou make it like to thine?
Sweet Lady of the Sacred Heart,
    Hear my fond prayer;
Thy calm, approving smile impart,
    Or I despair.

Those heavenly eyes are kindly turned;
They rest upon my aching heart.
Ah! Mary, once again I've learned
How more than merciful thou art!
For in no age hath anyone
    Implored thy aid,
But thy most tender will was done,
    God's anger stayed.

SISTER M. IGNATIA

THE CONQUERED

Dawn has her habitation in the sun.
Come from an ancient lineage of days,
She walks on steeps of light. In all her ways
She is serenely beautiful. Undone,
Wind-smoothed, her cloud of hair flows gold, and one
Low star she wears upon her breast. She stays
The rustling leaves, strewn petals, skylark-lays
With miracles unending, unbegun.

I lie, a flower unpetaled for her feet;
I call, a bird that neither sings nor flies,
Caught in the wisps of gold that are her hair.
I fall, a leaf of silver, joy-replete.
I die, a star gone pallid with her eyes,
Oppressed with beauty I can never bear.

SISTER MARY IMMACULATE

FILFILLMENT

You ask if I possess You with delight.
Beloved, yes; but let me tell You first
How I possess You wholly and yet thirst;
Repletely and yet hunger; solely, height
Past reach, nor compass You; with what frail might
Divinely I possess You as I durst,
And humanly, as Bread. In You immersed,
I hold You, Love, as one possesses light.

And with delight are You possessed, adored?
Oh, who shall set a depth to Your great sea,
Or bound the sky's infinity of blue,
Or measure space beyond the stars, my Lord?
Beloved, past all limits that there be
Is this delight: my joy possessing You.

SISTER MARY IMMACULATE

ORDINATION

You have no mortal lineaments this day.
In eyes where once I saw my own, I find
The soul of God, my son. I cannot bind
Your strength; no sinews that I gave can stay
Nor compass it. My fetters must give way
Before all might, and flesh my love designed
To love's infinity: a sign is signed
Indelibly with Spirit on this clay.

Yet you are mine, my son! I walked a far
Deep valley seeking you and showed your wild
Young feet this pilgrimage. What shall I dread
When you lead home, whence all our questings are?
Your eyes my light, your strength my staff, O child!
And for my hunger, you will give me Bread.

SISTER MARY IMMACULATE

BIRD ON A WINTER TREE

I SAW a tree against an austere sky
Raise barren arms this cold, white winter day.
Where shadowed snow more still than silence lay,
One small gray bird, too tremulous to fly,
Pressed close, and sang to it again the high
Uncadenced melody of gathered May.
Could song sweep years and loneliness away?
I listened with the tree, one knowing why.

Unsmitten yet by winter, I shall sing
A blossomed song to you when beauty wanes,
And quickened, sudden, you shall know to start
Through dawn-blue shadows everlasting spring.
One day I heard it singing in your veins;
Held close, I felt it throbbing in your heart.

SISTER MARY IMMACULATE

THE VALIANT

THIS rain-washed twilight world is not a blur
Of mist and trees; horizons are unrolled
In tones of blue, and veins of virgin gold
Have been unskyed where depths of storm clouds were.
White winds, expectant, hold their breath, nor stir.
As from forgotten embers, day flames bold,
Then dies. Night finds no pallor to enfold,
No vagueness in the moon that follows her.

You are that flower unshattered by the wet
Cold fingers of the early wind; that leaf
Which spans its autumn on the moon; that bird
Which on the gold has dared its silhouette.
You are a flame that challenges all grief
Where neither voice nor languages are heard.

SISTER MARY IMMACULATE

COUNTRY ROADS IN MAY

Over the meadows, new-starred with spring blossoms,
  Young April fled weeping away;
From distant horizon, with purple haze misted,
  She smiled through her tears, and today
Showers of gold buttercups bloom in her footsteps
  And brighten the roadsides of May.

She hung on the boughs of the trees, ere departing,
  The garlands she wore in her hair;
Through woodland and meadow she spilled the sweet
      perfume
  Of fresh-opened flowers, and there
Where the roadsides in May wind like ribbons of silver
  She scattered blue violets fair.

Young April has vanished, but back from the hillsides
  Her soft, mocking laughter rings still,
And cardinal and oriole echo its music
  In bird-song delightful, until
Every roadside in May where young April fled weeping
  With rapture of spring is athrill.

SISTER M. IMELDINE

A ROSARY

I HAVE a rosary of memories,
Strung bead by bead upon the white gold of the years,
I tell it over in the star-lit dusk, remembering
    With my tears.

Echoes of laughter lilting across shadows,
Songs of forgotten days and fragments of broken dreams,
Faces as dim and haunting as moonlight silvering
    Quiet streams.

Memories of woodlands where spring flung her flowers,
And every golden autumn blazed her glorious trail,
Hillsides embroidered in purple shadows under winter's
    Frosty veil.

As dusted rose leaves in a quaint old jar
Hold all the sweetness of long-faded garden flowers,
So on my rosary of memories are strung
    Forgotten hours.

SISTER M. IMELDINE

THE MENDICANT DIVINE

HE COMES at morning when the sleepy stars at last
Have sunk to rest, and fast
In slumber lie upon the breast of day.
The rose and gold and gray
Embroidered veil of dawn is flung aside
To greet the sun, and so is opened wide
The doorway of my soul, upon whose threshold
There is set a-shine
Love's welcoming fire for Him Who begs my heart,
The Mendicant divine.

And oh, at evening when the long blue shadows fall
Upon the world, and all
The homing birds wing happily to rest;
When far across the west,
The flaming candle of the setting sun
Glows from the window sill of heaven, then one
By one the love-lit stars of all my yearning thoughts
Are set a-shine
For Him Who begs the harvest of my day,
The Mendicant divine.

SISTER M. IMELDINE

THE GROTTO STEPS

How many years are gone since you were made,
  Gray steps down which so many feet have passed;
Over your stones the rain and sun have played
  And wintry blast!

Pilgrim and brother press you as they go,
  Full weary, to the stillness of the shrine.
Sweet, laughing children, age with footsteps slow,
  All these are thine.

How many hearts when passing down the stair,
  At Mary's feet seek comfort and release
From pain, and having left their burden there,
  Pass up in peace!

SISTER M. IMELDINE

61

TABLEAUX

I HOLD Him as His mother held Him, close
Against my heart to shut all else from sight.
I play with Him the way the children played
Within the village warm with morning light.

I smile upon Him much as Joseph smiled
To see the kindness of this thoughtful Child.

Like Peter, John, I walk with Him the roads
That burn in noonday sun our eager feet.
We stop to rest at Sichar's favored well;
We pluck the grape, the yellow grains of wheat.

Often He speaks to those one might condemn,
While I in secret kiss His garment's hem.

At last, alone, I climb a destined hill,
And weeping, seek Him when the night is gone;
Then, as to her who loved Him much, He comes
To make for me another Easter dawn.

SISTER M. JOHN FREDERICK

JOCULATOR DOMINI

"God give you peace!" Your happy lai
Won all to your pacific sway:
  Cathari, Guelf and Ghibelline
  Forswore the wonted battle scene
To learn a simple roundelay.

Your friends, the birds, were apt, they say,
In singing it the proper way.
  How glad their chorus must have been:
  "God give you peace!"

God's troubadour, on earth today
The ways of men would quite gainsay
  Such songs as yours. No more is seen
  The peace of poverty, your queen.
Teach us who had forgot to pray:
  "God give you peace!"

                    SISTER M. JOHN FREDERICK

WAITING

The long, impatient days drag on slow feet
Before the eager whip of my desire;
My heart, too glad for earth, with love on fire,
Finds all creation new, divinely sweet.
Above, below, beneath, within, I meet
Love tokens ravishing. All things conspire
To raise my eager heart to something higher,
Until in longing I must fain retreat!

Hide from my eyes the beauty of Your face
Soft-mirrored in the loveliness of earth.
Let no bird sing of Your enrapturing grace,
Lest I guess more of Your supernal worth
Than joy-brimmed heart can bear and men should say:
She died of love before profession day.

SISTER M. LEONELLA

CANDLES BEFORE YOUR FACE

WHITE candles we have lighted, Lord, that they
May shine from humble hill and mountain height
To mark Your dwellings in the world. Alight
With love, they feed on white simplicity.
The wax of youth was molded in Your way
For tapers tall, whose steady flames are bright
Against the darkness of indifferent night
And hostile winds that threaten youth's fair day.

From prayer and work we watch with eager eyes
Our lighted candles glowing through the years.
We pray, sweet Lady, guard them from the skies,
Lest golden flames should falter and grow dim;
O Virgin pure, whose white soul magnifies
The light of life, tend these young lights for Him.

SISTER M. LUCY

BEECH TREES

I PASSED a wood of beech trees yesterday
And I am shaken with its beauty yet.
Why should my breath catch and my eyes be wet
Because a hundred trees some yards away
Know simply how to dress in simple gray,
Are poised beyond the need of epithet,
And beautiful past power to forget?
I dare not think how they will look in May.

They wore illustrious yellow in the fall.
Their beauty is no thing at which they guess.
And when they put on green, and when they carry
Fans open in the sun or folded small,
I'll look through tears at ultimate loveliness:
Beeches in May, beeches in February.

SISTER M. MADELEVA

THE YOUNG PRIEST'S MOTHER

Yes, he is mine if miracles of weaving
Flesh from my flesh and blood into the fine
Potencies of white manhood, every line
Perfect past mute desire or proud believing
Can make him; if the mystery of achieving
Out of a human son this son divine
Owes aught to motherhood, then he is mine
Beyond my body's gift, my soul's conceiving.

And I am his beyond the extremest guesses
Of men, bound by indissoluble bands
Forever. It is not only he who blesses
And holds me close, but oh, he understands
Why adoration burns in my caresses,
What wounds I kiss upon his beautiful hands!

SISTER M. MADELEVA

PENELOPE

Penelope never has raveled as I have raveled;
She never has fashioned the fabrics that I have spun;
And neither her heart nor her lover has traveled as mine
 has traveled
Under the sun.

Her web of delay, deliberate, passionate, splendid,
Was tense with allurement, I doubt not; was wet with
 tears;
But love found it raveled, unfinished — a burial robe —
 and ended
Those piteous years.

My fingers run wildly through warps of bewildering
 wonder,
Or dream over woof of caught silence or sudden song;
They tighten on patterns of laughter or fear that is
 stricken thunder! —
O love, how long?

Is it naught that I pause in my web as yon suitor woos me;
That I ravel at night with regret the design of day;
That loneliness sickens, grief dazes, and doubt pursues me
With you away?

With a lifetime of years do I lash myself to you and
      bind you,
Do I dare all the seas of the world without compass or
      star;
Past the lands of Calypso and Circe and Scylla I seek
      you and find you,
Be it never so far!

So I fare on the deific pathway my love has traveled
As I fashion the web that Penelope could not have spun,
And ravel the heavenly robe of delay that she could not
      have raveled
Under the sun.

SISTER M. MADELEVA

A QUESTION OF LOVERS

THERE be lovers who bring me roses, the velvet of buds
    upcurled;
But only one lover gives me the blossoms of all the world.

There be those who have pearls, have rubies; but much
    as I care for these,
This night will my true love bring me the moon and the
    Pleiades.

I have tokens, if gifts could buy me, till love and its quest
    be done.
Who will catch me a cloud's white splendor; who will
    fetch me the dying sun?

Or who, on the wings of the morning, will hasten, when
    dawn is sweet,
To meet and possess me solely? One only, with piercéd
    feet.

And who, for he loves me truly, will give me as token this,
This poignance of love unspoken, two wounds in his
    hands to kiss?

SISTER M. MADELEVA

70

A NUN SPEAKS TO MARY

I

IN THE DAYS OF KING HEROD

You had no little maid, so I remember,
To help you sweep and tidy up the room,
To sit and watch with you that first December
Through shining twilights deep with golden gloom.

Through all those wistful days you had no mother
To know your wonder and to share your joy
Of fashioning — you could not let another! —
The darling swaddling garments for your Boy.

There was not any housewife to befriend you
The day word came to go to Bethlehem town;
No kinswoman bethought her to attend you
Of all the folk of David going down.

And when you held Him to your heart in wonder,
Emmanuel, God's Son, your Boy, the Word
Made flesh Who shook the skies with holy thunder,
In Bethlehem not any mother stirred.

A NUN SPEAKS TO MARY

II

SEQUEL

Now come again the sweet Isaian days,
Merciful, tender;
I know their loneliness; I dream their splendor.
Down their plain ways,
Mary, I come,
Confounded with this former shame, and dumb.
Take me in service, in complete surrender,
Waking and sleeping;
Take every daily task; take every duty;
Take little homely things as dusting, sweeping;
Change them into your heavenly housekeeping;
Touch them with Nazareth's most stricken beauty.
Think that my busy hands weave raiment fair
For Christ to wear;
Know that my hurrying feet
Run all your errands, Sweet;
And should they tarry,
Hear how I promise them,
My Lady Mary,
That they at length may go with you to Bethlehem.

And at the last let be
On those three mute and piteous, fearful days
When none of all earth's womenfolk is near you,
That you will have to help you and to cheer you
In little foolish ways
Poor, simple me;
That when you stand outside the inn, the night wind
        blowing,
I will be there
Adoring, knowing;
That if the whole wide world should have no room,
I will be waiting through whatever gloom
To be your resting place. But this is heaven I dare!

So, let my promise be my prayer.
And do not seek for any cave at all
With patient kine and manger crib and stall
Beyond the gates of little Bethlehem town
To lay your dear Son down.
Mother all fair,
Lay Him within my hungry arms to sleep;
Lay Him within my hungry heart to keep,
Adorable, holy,
Little and lowly.
And let earth's shepherds, let heaven's seraphim
So find me with you Christmas night, adoring, loving Him.

SISTER M. MADELEVA

RIDDLES ONE, TWO, AND THREE

MY LOVER is a fool more wise
Than Solomon;
My lover is a bird that flies
Into the sun.

He is a lighted lamp, my love,
A midnight cry,
A mortal worm that died to prove
He could not die.

My lover is a cedar tree
With branches spread;
A sweet and bitter fruit is he,
Alive and dead.

My lover is a quiet rain
Falling on fleece;
My lover is or endless pain
Or endless peace,

Or sometime an instinctive mole
Breaking the clod;
My lover is a thief who stole
The name of God.

SISTER M. MADELEVA

74

OLD SOLDIERS

Look at this avenue. Do you not love it,
This regiment of trees in ranks of fours
Marching abreast, maples and sycamores?
It is a bodyguard a king could covet.
I like its strength, but most, the beauty of it,
And this one thing too mere for metaphors,
Its gray-black-white with winter out-of-doors,
And any winter sky at all above it.

There is one austere veteran; you must know him,
That grave, gaunt sycamore, battered and white
And standing stark beneath the blue of noon.
What a fine debt of dignity we owe him!
But wait until you watch him through the night;
Wait till you see him sharp against the moon.

SISTER M. MADELEVA

YOU ASK MY AGE

I AM older than dawn
And sunset are.
I can think past the light
Of the oldest star.

The piled-up mountains
And ancient trees,
Timeless rivers
And ageless seas;

East and west winds,
South and north:
I know the hour
That brought them forth.

How old am I?
As days are told,
The earth is younger
Than I am old.

Years cannot measure
Time for me.
Fetch us the clock
Of infinity.

This is the answer
If you would know;
From life I come;
To life I go.

Wherefore I am
More gladly young
Than a child not born,
Than a song not sung;

More young than the spring
Before its birth,
Than the dreaming life
In the dreaming earth;

More young than the hosts
Of seraphim
Who sing, "Hosanna,
Elohim."

Older I am
Than any star
And younger than
The angels are.

SISTER M. MADELEVA

CHRISTMAS:

Elizabeth Watches the Night Sky

I THINK the clouds tonight
Are lambs and wayward sheep,
Huddled and lost and white.
My boy stirs in his sleep!

At midnight he awoke
As at an uttered word.
I only guess who spoke
And what he heard.

His eyes, before he slept,
Grew deep as prophets' are.
Up from their darkness leapt
Light like a star.

Two clouds drift in the blue.
How strangely moved I am!
They are like a lone ewe
And her young lamb.

SISTER M. MADELEVA

QUESTIONS ON A NUN'S HABIT

You do not think it is because I do not share
A woman's subtle weakness for the piquancy of dress,
Its swift, sure coquetry, its studied carelessness,
That I wear what I wear?
You do not think it is because I do not dare
Its recklessness?
What do you say
Of wearing one's bridal gown
To town,
To church on Good Friday?
Of wearing one's shroud
Every day, all day,
In the heat and the crowd,
On Easter and Christmas day?
You do not tell me that I have bad taste,
Or none at all, or that I am less than fastidious and proud.
Is it because you do not wish to waste
Words upon one whose world in secret you deplore?
You are not sorry for me.
You do not think me dressed quite unbecomingly?
(You would give much to be attired so adequately?)
Of all the dozen gowns I ever wore
And have abandoned, orchid and shadow-gray and
      powder-blue,
This is the only one that you need envy me.
— You have not ever cared to find me beautiful before,
Have you?

SISTER M. MADELEVA

79

JEWELRY

Pearls such as yours a proud queen quaffed one day;
A jealous queen such diamonds flung away;
Your ring once Portia might have haggled for
Your bracelets finer are than Esther wore.

A queen brought me my beads from Nazareth,
Egypt and Judah; she was done to death
Almost in fetching them. What bitterness
She bore, from this cross you, perhaps, can guess.

Her only Son was nailed upon it — see,
Jesus of Nazareth, on Calvary;
And this inscription Pilate fastened there.
Beads are the only jewelry I wear.

SISTER M. MADELEVA

GATES

THE oranges at Jaffa gate
Are heaped in hills; men sell and buy
Or sit and watch the twisted road
Or David's tower against the sky.

The Golden Gate is walled with stone.
No king can pass nor prophet see
The valley of Jehosaphat,
The olives of Gethsemane.

St. Stephen's is a quiet gate,
A simple door that lets in dawn.
Its hill, its walls, its ancient stones,
What strange things they have looked upon!

Asses, belabored, stumble past;
Traffickers clamor; priests debate;
A child begs alms; a blind man gropes
To sunshine at Damascus gate.

The world has narrow gates and wide;
Men seek their loves through all of them;
And I have come here, seeking mine,
Jerusalem, Jerusalem!

SISTER M. MADELEVA

MEDITATION ON ATLAS

ATLAS held the firmament
But could not see the sun;
He had the world between his hands
But did not have its fun.

He ate the bread of bitterness
Nor knew that bread is sweet;
Nor guessed the joy of outstretched arms,
The gayety of feet.

The earth was on his shoulders;
The sky was on the earth;
He did not know its wonder;
He did not know its mirth.

He knelt for aeons, burdened
With the whole unwieldy scheme,
And he missed the point entirely
Of the grand, deific theme.

I have hung for years together
On a stark, two-branching tree.
It holds the earth and sky apart;
It binds them endlessly.

My tree becomes a table;
I have tasted of its food;
I have eaten of God's body;
I have dared to drink God's blood.

I am stretched out and uplifted
Among stars and planets piled,
In the anguish of the prophets
And the weakness of a child.

I can hold the earth for Atlas
And the skies above his head;
I can hold the God Who made them
And He will not strike me dead.

Be strong and glad as God is;
Open your great arms wide
And set your feet against God's feet,
Atlas. Be crucified.

SISTER M. MADELEVA

LOVELY THINGS

I SHALL remember lovely things:
The thrilling joy when a bluebird wings
Its way through the dusk of eventide
To a quiet tree on the mountain side;
The dainty flit of a butterfly;
The delicate blue of a drifting sky;
The silent call of the evening star;
The rose's perfume wafted far.
I shall remember lovely things:
A smile, a tear, a heart that sings.

SISTER M. NOEL

MEDITATION

As DIED in crimson flame the sunset glow,
Adown the golden pathway of the west
We strayed, my heart and I, in search of rest
Where blooms the edelweiss beneath the snow.
There on the height, far from the ebb and flow
Of ocean tide, niched in the mountain's crest,
A dawn-tinged shell I found, and as I prest
It to my ear, it murmured sweet and low

Of far-off deeps whose rhythmic rise and swell
Lulled it to slumber 'neath the amber foam.
Ah! would, dear God, my heart like that fair shell,
Through morning sunlight and the evening gloam,
Though far apart from Thee it needs must dwell,
Might sing forever of its heavenly home.

SISTER M. OLGA

SAINT VINCENT DE PAUL

O SOLDIER of Christ, who manfully trod
The pathway to freedom — the footsteps of God!
What treasures are thine in the mansions of rest,
The kingdom of glory, the home of the blest!
What rays from the throne encompass thee now;
What beautiful diadem circles thy brow!
For, glorious saint, 'twas thine arm unfurled
The banner of charity over the world!

O friend of the orphan, O help of the weak,
'Twas thy hand that wiped the tear from the cheek
Of sorrow and suffering, while binding with care
The wounds of the soul with the balsam of prayer.
O glorious saint, thy mission has spread
Its wings o'er the earth — by the fever-fanned bed
Thy daughters are kneeling — for dearer than all
Were the hearts of the suffering to Vincent de Paul.

SISTER M. PAULINE

PIETA

I HAVE a little song for you,
A golden song and gay,
To soothe your sword-pierced mother heart
And fold your fears away.

I have a little song for you,
As wistful as the rain,
Cool fingertips against your brow,
White peace to ease your pain.

I have a little song for you,
Ah, mother, hear me then,
And as you kiss the lips of Christ,
Remember me. Amen.

SISTER M. PHILIP

PSALM

I

MY LOVE for You is the scent of sage
　　After a summer shower . . .
Or a yellow birch in the pale gold sunlight
　　Of an autumn afternoon . . .
Sometimes a mountain flaming with October . . .
Then suddenly, a cedar heaped with snow.

II

Your love for me, O God,
　　Is sun
　　And rain,
　　Frost
　　And snow.

III

Your love for me, O God, is a tree
　　With far-flung arms . . .
And Your Body — a broken flower . . .
A strong cry of agony —
　　With silence the only answer . . .
Magdalen, Peter, and John . . .
And Mary, my mother, forever. . . .

SISTER M. PHILIP

WINTER DUSK

Winter dusk and a world of snow;
Beauty that takes my breath!
God, are they always hand in hand,
Loveliness and death?

SISTER M. PHILIP

POET'S BREAD

HUNGER is a
Poet's bread,
So never a poet but
Goes well fed.

If poet's bread were
Poet's pay,
Many a one would
Starve on the way.

But poets sing
While thin-lipped years
Make hunger-bread of
Beauty and tears.

SISTER M. PHILIP

AUTUMN PRAYER

You Who have painted
The hillsides gold
And colored the trees
With flame,
Touch my life
With Your dear smile;
My heart
With Your loved name.

SISTER M. PHILIP

BROTHER STICK

BROTHER FRANCIS, turn your eyes
From the hills of paradise
To the cell of Brother Stick,
For my heart is dull and sick.
Kindle it with your desire
(Dry wood makes the best of fire.)
For, my Brother, I would fain
That none of Stick, but Love, remain.
Look on me with shining eyes
From the hills of paradise!
Seraph Heart, so young and quick,
Hear and answer Brother Stick.

SISTER M. PHILIP

TODAY

Today my thoughts
Are swift and cool
As goldfish in
A lily pool.

Tomorrow, like as not,
They'll be
Brown turtles blinking
Hard at me.

And I shall be
As dull as they
And blink back, too.
But oh, today!

SISTER M. PHILIP

CHRISTMAS

Soft gleams of radiant light
Fall from the distant skies;
Glorias wing their flight
To a crib where an Infant lies.
Glory to God in the highest
Thrills the heavens afar;
Glory to God in the highest
Sings the new-born star.

SISTER M. PRUDENTIANA

NIGHT FROM THE NURSERY

A CRUST of moon
Goes sailing by
Within the milky
Rim of sky,
And crumbs of stars
Come tumbling down
Upon the carpet
Of the town.

SISTER M. RAPHAELITA

PROPRIETY

I NEVER like tea roses
At Joseph's feet;
They seem effeminate,
Too sweet
For such a man as he.
Today some pussy willows,
Stately and tall,
Made silver etchings
On the wall
Around his shrine.
And he seemed pleased,
I thought,
That someone fitting tribute
For a man
Had brought.

SISTER M. RAPHAELITA

96

HILLTOPS

Some love a crested peak
Outlined against the sky,
And some for awe can scarcely gaze
At great cliffs towering high.
I love the little hills
Somber and shy,
Who dare not, in their littleness,
Touch the hem of sky.

SISTER M. RAPHAELITA

LILIES OF THE VALLEY

Soft your bells of pearl are ringing,
On the air sweet fragrance flinging,
　　Lovely lilies of the vale,
Maytime's dainty blossoms frail,
　　Gladness bringing,
　　Graceful, swinging,
Snow-white lilies of the vale.

You are like that lovely flower,
Brought to earth from heaven's bower,
　　Fairest lily ever seen,
Mother chaste of gracious mien.
　　Hearts are singing,
　　Praises bringing
To sweet Mary, heaven's queen.

SISTER M. RESURRECTION

THE HERALD

A ROLLICKSOME fellow is bold Sir March;
Not a bit of respect has he
For bird or flower, oak or larch,
Or the daintiest things that be.

He scatters the gray when the clouds hang low,
And coaxes the sunshine through;
Then all of a sudden, down falls the snow
And gone is the sky's bright blue.

He shouts and roars in the writhing trees,
Or whistles a tender lay
In accents soft to the waking leaves,
Then, mocking, runs away.

Let him frolic away to his heart's content;
We know he but paves the way;
We know that he has one sweet intent,
To hasten Saint Joseph's day.

SISTER M. RESURRECTION

THE FIRST OF APRIL

In her Christmas robe, just dropped from heaven,
I saw the earth this morn at seven,
And winter in state on his throne.

A soft note high from a white-branched tree
Called down to the very heart of me;
I looked and a cardinal's breast flashed red
As it darted sunward over my head.

"Thus passes the glory of winter," I said,
"For spring has come into her own."

SISTER M. REYNALDE

THE ETERNAL JUBILEE

(For Sister Bethania)

THE book is now all written to the end;
The chain full rounded with the mystic seal
Of love in death. Now soft our Aves blend
With joy-bells that from heavenly towers peal.
For as the first faint star in evening sky
Gladdens the heart, so as the angels peer
Into God's galaxy of saints, they spy
An aureole new, shining out golden clear.
Then all the starlit vaults of heaven ring
With angel psaltery and joyful lay
For that the bride has come unto the King
To dwell with Him forever and for aye.

SISTER M. REYNALDE

SUNSET AT NOTRE DAME

THE shadow-surpliced trees are acolytes
  Before a host of fire;
The gathering opal clouds are incense-praise;
  The homing birds, the choir.

Across the emerald lake a path of gold
  Leads to the temple stair,
And on the stillness falls a silver sound,
  The evening bell for prayer.

God's blessing is upon the silent land;
  The mystic rite is o'er;
The tabernacle of the day is closed
  And night has sealed the door.

When lo! swung out by angel hands,
  Behold a gleam afar,
The jeweled sanctuary lamp of night,
  The faithful evening star!

SISTER M. RITA

FROM DARK TO LIGHT

Out of the purple night
  Cometh the light,
Building a golden way
  For a new day.
So, when the last dread hour
  O'er me shall lower,
Grant that the dark shall be
  A way to Thee.

SISTER M. RITA

ON HEARING A BELL TOLL

SOME day the bell I hear
  My death shall toll;
And when the moment strikes,
  What of my soul?

What then shall all avail
  That now I prize,
When clear the misspent past
  Before me lies?

What then shall be the worth
  Of human praise,
That sheds a glory now
  Along life's ways?

What then of all the friends
  I now hold dear?
Remembrance all too oft
  Dies at the bier.

O when that solemn bell
  My death shall toll,
For me there shall but count
  God and my soul!

SISTER M. RITA

TILL THE HARVEST DAYS

THOU hast plowed, dear God, the field of my heart;
  The furrows are traced in pain;
Thou hast sown the seed, and to make them start,
  Thou hast showered my tears for rain.

Thou hast stirred the deeps with love's fruitful rays,
  The rays of a love divine;
Do Thou guard the field till the harvest days,
  For the field and the fruit are Thine!

SISTER M. RITA

SISTERS OF THE HOLY CROSS

Jerusalem beheld the cross divine
   Uplifted, where her children all might see
   The outstretched branches of the fruitful tree,
From which was spilled redemption's precious wine.
It gleamed across the dawn, and Constantine
   Before its glory bent his royal knee,
     A fairer conquest than the victory,
Then promised through the power of that sign.

With all the majesty of Calvary's hill,
   And all the glory of the Roman sky,
     Unchanged in promise of a gain in loss,
The sacred sign leads on an army still;
   O'er all this western land its pennants fly,
     The army of the Sisters of the Cross.

SISTER M. RITA

COMING OF THE WORD

JUDEA saw
A maiden beautiful,
All grace and happiness,
Run out to meet the molten morning sun.

She stood upon the rim of day and night:
Behind, all darkness,
And before, all light.

The Holy Three
Drew sudden near,
A perfect soul's all-perfect prayer to hear.
They loved the virgin well,
And missioned Gabriel
With message for the maid.

How long she prayed
Sweet Mary never knew.
A child she knelt;
A woman grown, she rose;
For she had heard
The Word.

SISTER M. ROSE GERTRUDE

IT NEEDS MUST BE

You wish for other Christs:
Then marvel not
At Herod being near;
At Pilate washing hands as red as blood;
A taunt; a jeer.
Could Christ be bound without a binding hand?
Could He be crucified without command?

SISTER M. ROSE GERTRUDE

OLD LACE

Marvelous fabric of price never spoken,
    Lace of an ivory hue;
Into it woven dreams that are broken,
    Hopes that never came true.

Intricate pattern no artist could trace,
    Delicate lines in a grandmother's face;
Memory's treasure no time can efface,
    Priceless old ivory lace.

SISTER M. ROSE GERTRUDE

LUX ET TENEBRAE

How far away
Is night from day?

I read a marvel
Of a wondrous light
One bright midnight,
Where two, distressed,
Found rest
Within a cave.

And then I read
Of clouds like lead
That rumbled with despair
Up in the mountain there.
They blackened the bright sun
Till none
Could see his hand before his face.
Yes, Calvary was the place.
And men grew grave
And shook with fright
That noonday night.

SISTER M. ROSE GERTRUDE

OUR LADY'S ANTHEMS

WHEN earth her rest is taking,
And the leaves have ceased to fall;
When birds in distant woodlands
To their mates no longer call;
When the days of Advent bid us
For our Saviour's birth prepare,
Then the sweet strains of the Alma
Float upon the vesper air.
Mater, Mater Redemptoris,
Tender mother, friend most true,
Peccatorum miserere,
We place all our hope in you.

When the Christmastide is ended,
And the Lenten days draw near;
When the shadow of our errors
Seems to fall more dark and drear;
When our hearts are bowed in sorrow
For the woes which we have wrought
Unto Him Who loved us truly
And our souls with life-blood bought;
Then comes, like the dawn of morning,
Dawn dispelling grief's thick shade,
Ave, Regina coelorum,
Hail to thee, O glorious maid!

When the earth in radiant beauty
Dons her new springtime attire,
And the flowers are all in blossom,
And the birds with songs inspire;
Then the Church in joyous gladness
Dries the penitential tear,
Tells us now to leave our sadness
For our risen Lord is near.
List ye, list ye to the singing,
It was ne'er so grand as now.
Regina coeli, laetare!
At thy feet we humbly bow.

When the summer heat is glowing,
And the breezes scarcely move,
And the thirsty cattle lowing,
Gather in the shady grove;
When our fainting hearts grow weary
Of the world's deluding dross,
And we pine for soul's perfection
Even while we dread the cross;
Then Salve Regina cheers us,
Lifts on high our tear-dimmed eyes
To our Mater Misericordiae
Beyond the cloud-flecked skies.

MOTHER M. SIENNA

TO A CHILD AT FIRST COMMUNION
(*For Eleanore*)

AN ANGEL'S hand, I fancy, snatched the blue
From heaven's azure depths to form those eyes.
I love them best when full of glad surprise
Their gaze meets mine. Sweet Innocence, 'tis you
Alone can stamp with beauty ever new
The mortal brow. Your mystic charm close lies
Around the young, still near to God. Disguise
Of sin alone can hide the spirit's view.

Dear God, from out my heart I plead today
Guard Thou those eyes and fix their light on Thee.
Let not a sinful world their gaze allure,
Nor let them e'er be dimmed with sin's decay.
Sweet eyes of blue, O may you ever be
Deep springs of innocence and love most pure.

MOTHER M. VINCENTIA

FOR CHRIST AND HOLY CROSS
(*For Mother Augusta*)

THIS humble tribute hers, whose life-span knew
The griefs of earth. Deluded not by fame
That weaklings crave, unswayed by scathing blame,
Life's dominant in her rang ever true.
Her strength, as warrior saints of old, she drew
From Christ for Holy Cross. Could higher aim
With courage born of heaven, heart inflame?
A Judith brave, she led the valiant few.

We need the lessons of thy selfless life
To weigh the gold of heaven against earth's dross;
To hold Christ's standard high as swift years roll.
Ah! may our hearts through time's unceasing strife
Prove like to thine, thou daughter of the cross,
As true to God as needle is to pole.

                                    MOTHER M. VINCENTIA

SACERDOS IN AETERNUM

GREAT Angelo unto stone gave breath,
And Raphael's glowing canvas knows not death.
Sweet harmony a spell throws o'er the heart,
But here is power beyond the touch of art!

A miracle is here, a power sublime,
Divinely writ upon the scroll of time.
But yesterday in humble paths he trod;
Today, a priest, from heaven he calls God.

MOTHER M. VINCENTIA